DISCOVER YOUR SPIRITUALITY

JEANNE HINTON

To Brother Bernard ssf, Carolyn Reinhart and Geraldine O'Meara of the Post Green Pastoral Centre, and to the Sisters of the Commaunate of Grandchamp in Switzerland, whose wisdom and support have helped me to discover more about myself.

Copyright © 1992 Hunt & Thorpe
Text © 1992 by Jeanne Hinton
Illustrations © 1992 by Len Munnik
Originally published by Hunt & Thorpe 1992

ISBN 1 85608 105 2

In Australia this book is published by:
Hunt & Thorpe Australia Pty Ltd.
9 Euston Street, Rydalmere NSW 2116

A CIP catalogue record for this book is available from
the British Library

Manufactured in the United Kingdom

CONTENTS

*Spirituality is
like living water
that springs up in
the very depths of
the experience
of faith.*

Gustavo Gutierrez

■ INTRODUCTION

Each day faces us with new decisions; some small, some big.

There are decisions to make about what to eat; what to wear, whether to accept an invitation, to spend the evening watching television, reading a book or mowing the grass.

There may be decisions we take on behalf of others, at home or at work. We may be faced with a big decision that is going to have longterm consequences: to accept a job, to move house, to marry or to break off a relationship. Some may be decisions of consequence: to take a stand against an injustice, to refuse compromise or deceit.

The decisions we make say a lot about our values, our attitude to life and the meaning we give to relationships and to material things. In other words, they say something about our spirituality. Spirituality is a word that describes that part of ourselves that lies deepest within, that influences our decisions and the course of our life – hidden, yet extremely powerful. A secular definition of 'spirit' is 'vital principle', 'actuating emotion, disposition, frame of mind'.[1] A more religious definition is 'inner spark' or 'life force'. Everyone has a spirituality, but not every person nourishes that part of their being. It is here too in the deepest part of our being that we can come to know God, who is Spirit.

This book is about discovering your spirituality. The exercises throughout are your aids to this journey of discovery. This is both a journey you make on your own and also with others. There are parts of the journey we can only make for and by ourselves, but we deceive ourselves if we think this is a journey we make wholly on our own. We are more connected than we know to all those who in the past have trodden out for us well loved and well used pathways, and also we are connected to all those who today are discovering anew a spirituality that is one for our times. And our own journey will connect us even closer to all these others – if the spirituality we are discovering and want to build on is wholesome and lifegiving for us and others. Anything else we will want to discard!

■ I

A DEEP WELL

SOMETIMES THE WORD 'spirituality' is used only a limited sense. It is used to describe a person's relationship to God, but it is more than this – it is about the way we relate to the whole of life. One's spirituality is like a deep well of accumulated values and experiences from which one draws wisdom and strength for the various tasks and decisions of everyday life.

'Everyone,' said St. Bernard of Clairvaux, 'has to drink from his own well.' Not everything that is accumulated in this well is helpful, but in it there are hidden treasures that can be a source of life and energy. The water in this well is not static.

Whether we are conscious of it or not, we are continually being shaped and reshaped in our inner being. To clear the well of what is unhelpful from time to time is essential for growth and healing. And unless we dig for the hidden treasures within, much may lie dormant

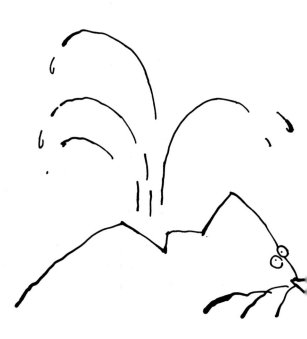

and unused. That is why it is important to know as much as we can about our particular inner well or spirituality.

It is here in this deepest part of our being that our unique self is being formed, that part of ourselves that Christians believe lives on after the mind has ceased to function, and the body has died. It is here too within this deepest part of our being that questions about the meaning of life – and of each of our lives in particular – are answered.

Here is a simple exercise to help you apply this to your own life. You can complete it in fifteen to thirty minutes.

• Think of the last time you made a major decision that had longterm consequences for your life. What were the factors that led you to make that decision? What does your decision tell you about your personal values; *about what matters to you*? Write three or four sentences in answer to these questions.

• Reflect on what you have written. Underline key words or phrases. These words are a starting place for discovering your spirituality.

■ 2

LIFE SCRIPTS

HOW ARE WE to discover what is hidden deep within? Psychologists tell us that most of us only realise twenty to thirty per cent or less of our full capacity. That means we each have a hidden potential of some seventy to eighty per cent – hidden talents, hidden possibilities of growth in being and in relating. That potential is in the hidden part of us, the part that we need to bring to consciousness. This is a lifelong task, but the steps along the way are steps any one of us can take. First, what is needed is the desire to start the journey, and some time for quiet thought and reflection.

What lies deepest within us has its roots in our past. Not only in our personal past, but that of our family going back generations, itself also influenced by the culture around. None of us lives our life in a vacuum. R L Stevenson in his *Essays of the Road* wrote, 'The future is nothing, but the past is myself, my own history, the seed of my present thoughts, the mould of my present disposition.' Who we are today is a result of others' influences upon our lives, and also a result of our own free choices and decisions. It is our own free choices and decisions that shapes our uniqueness.

There are questions here that are important to consider. Where were you born? What year? What was life like for your parents at that time? What stories have they told you about that time in their lives? What do you know about that period of history: of local, national and global events?

What were the immediate influences upon your parents' lives: religious, cultural, familial, social, political? What mattered to them? What do you remember of that period of your life before school began? What was its mood? What memories come back, and what significance do they have for you now? If you were born between the years of 1950 and 1963, you were born at a time of post war affluence, a time when parents were determined that their children should have all the comforts and opportunities that they missed out on

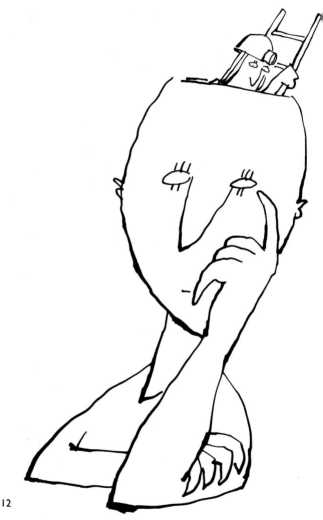

themselves in the war years. If you were born after that time, it is likely that your parents were into a more questioning frame of mind, influenced by the counter culture of those years.

I was born in Wales in the thirties, a time of deep depression. I am still discovering the depths to which that has influenced and formed me. The chart on page 14 gives you an idea of the common social experience that has shaped life in Britain since 1900. Much of it stands for our common experience in the West, and from this example you can draw up your own chart of the part of the world in which you live. If in the East, it will look a little different!

There are other more personal influences to explore – influences from childhood and adolescent years that have helped form you as an adult. Who were the people who were influential – peers and others? At what point can you remember making a significant decision of your own that determined a direction you would take? What lay behind that decision?

I can remember my drama teacher at school advising me to drop out of the drama class. I was easily put down as a child by other's

Social experience by age or birth

Born	Age in '90	Common social experience
1900 – 1920	90 – 70	First World War
1920 – 1935	70 – 55	Inter-war depression
1935 – 1950	55 – 40	European tension; Second World War; Cold War
1950 – 1963	40 –27	Post war affluence; baby boom
1963 – 1970	27 – 20	Counter Culture
1970 – 1990	20 – 0	Post-industrialism; high unemployment; technological advance; communications revolution

comments about my appearance or ability, but this time I challenged my teacher's opinion of my potential, and made what I remember now as my first major life decision. I decided to stay put in the drama class. I was a star struck teenager, who spent a lot of her spare time at the theatre and cinema. The drama class was important to me. I discovered and my drama teacher discovered that I had a real gift for direction and stage management, and by the end of my time at school I was both managing and helping to direct the school plays. As a result one suggestion I was given for a career choice was a career in the theatre! Thinking about that decision to stay put in the drama class, I realise I do have a capacity (though somewhat deeply buried!) to rise to a challenge if the matter is important enough to me, and I am also encouraged to go on believing in my own gut sense of where my abilities lie.

The questions I have listed above are important questions for all of us, and in answering them we begin to discover what it is we carry with us in our well. Some of the answers will come to mind easily; others may be buried deep in the personal subconscious. Raising the questions will begin to help the answers surface. At a spirituality workshop a participant faced with the task of answering questions about the first five years of his life, complained, 'But I have never been able to remember anything from that period of my life.' The next morning he told us, 'I had the most amazing night. I woke part way through to a flood of memories.'

■ PERSONAL SCRIPTS

Another way to gain insight into our inner well is to think of our life as a book, film or play. What story does it tell? Who are the main characters? What chapters or scenes would you break it into? What title would you give it? Such a title could be a clue to a life script which you carry with you. A title such as 'Forlorn Hopes' says a lot in a few words. Again we need to ask the underlying questions. Where has this script come from? What has shaped it?

Try the following exercise.

Draw a line from O to the age you are now. It can be a straight line or a spiral. On this line mark down significant happenings and life changes. Against each make a note of the year and of your age at the time. You can then begin to 'script' your story, giving each phase or scene a short title. Finally view your life to date as a whole, and write down an overall title that comes to mind.

Take the first two scenes, and fill in some of your early history, using the questions already given as a tool to help you 'dig'. You may want to use words or instead of words, drawings or symbols.

At this stage you may want just to work on this exercise briefly, returning at a another time to work on it in greater depth.

WHO GOD IS

EARLY INFLUENCES WILL also have helped shape what you feel about God.

If your parents or other significant adults in your early life talked about God and to God, then God will have been real to you too. But what kind of God ? Do you feel you are special to God, someone he loves dearly and that he wants the very best for you? Is God one who protects you from danger, to whom you turn for comfort and understanding? Or is he perhaps a God who demands of you more than you can give, or expects of you standards impossible to sustain? Does he seem distant or close? For you or against you? An enabling or a threatening presence?

Margaret, a friend of mine, remembers how as a child she was frightened of thunderstorms. For her the thunder was God's anger, and anger at her. She felt at such times that she must have done something dreadfully wrong. God was someone she feared. One day, however, she was staying with her grandmother, and overheard her grandmother having a conversation with a person in the next room. She was talking about the family, and then Margaret heard her say, 'And when are you going to take me home?' Margaret realised that her grandmother was talking to God in a very natural and intimate way. That incident opened up new possibilities

for her. 'She introduced me to a much more loving and caring Father.'

The kind of shape God has for us an an adult has its roots in the past, in these early emotional experiences. This will be true even if a stated belief in God was not part of your early

upbringing. Parent figures in our lives are god-persons and colour our feelings and expectations about God, however certain or uncertain our belief in God's existence. For a person who has happy childhood memories of being fathered, the image of God as a heavenly Father fits well. On the other hand, to address God as Father is distressing to many people since their human experience of fatherhood may be of absence, distance or abuse.

When we begin to explore these issues , we touch on matters that are of enormous importance, often of greater importance than we realise. For example, to question the appropriateness of always addressing God in the masculine as 'he' rather than 'she' will raise a hornet's nest in almost any group of people - for and against! The intensity of each person's contributions to the discussion will soon reveal that here we are treading on highly defended and even forbidden ground. This is because childhood experiences of being parented or not parented, and ideas and beliefs about God, are closely connected with our own sense of personal worth and significance.

As we grow into adulthood, we will begin to decide for ourselves whether or not there is a God, and what kind of God we believe in. We may, however, work this out at a rational level, and not realise that emotionally we still carry around with us images from our childhood, some helpful, others not. At times, particularly at times of personal crisis, it is likely that it is these emotions that will control our responses, not our head. Integrating mind and emotions is part of the journey into wholeness that we all need to make.

An important part of this journey will be to open ourselves to the reality of who God is. While others do shape our image of God, the reality of God is quite other than this. God is larger and other than any of us can know or fully comprehend,. What we can know about God is what God reveals to us - in creation, through relationships, within ourselves, made as we are in God's image. God also makes himself known to us in the way he acts in human history in all the salvation events from creation up to and including our own times. And supremely he has revealed himself through the humanity of Jesus. It is a lifelong process to open ourselves to God as God really is, allowing our 'images' to be questioned and if necessary discarded.

My friend, Margaret, also recalls that as a child she was neither really impressed or inspired by the person of Jesus. 'I think it may have had something to do with the gallery of pictures on the kitchen wall all depicting a very weak and plastic Jesus. He wasn't someone I could go to in a crisis I felt, because he had such a lot of trouble with those Jews and they crucified him in the end. Well, if God couldn't look after himself, what chance had we!' Margaret is now a Sister of the Sisters of the Infant Jesus. Her sense of who Jesus is changed when she began to read the bible during her novitiate. 'In the scriptures I met a different Jesus to the one on the kitchen wall, one who walked among and was friends with the ordinary people of his day, especially those pushed to the margins, who weren't part of the system of things.' She began then to experience a growing desire to know this Jesus.

The biblical revelation of who God is shows

him to be a God who loves, who wants the best for people, who protects, sustains and comforts. But he is also a God who has expectations, who makes demands, who is sometimes seemingly absent, who does not always give protection from danger or sustenance in need.

To take only one aspect of this revelation of who God is, to isolate it and to build our own faith experience on it alone, is to live with a distorted image. But through and in all of this revelation of God is the strong message - that God's intention is to redeem and liberate, not to condemn and destroy. This is an important gauge for our own attitudes and approach to life - our spirituality.

Here are some questions to help you think about this? How do you think of God? What are the strongest images that come to mind? What stories in the bible are you most drawn to? Why? Has your understanding of who God is grown and developed over the years? If so, how has this happened? What have been the circumstances, the influences?

■ 4

SEASONS AND STAGES

THERE ARE SEASONS to our life: spring, summer, autumn, winter. Spring is the season of childhood and adolescence; summer of early adulthood; autumn of middle adulthood and winter that of late adulthood. In theories of human development, there are ages that approximate to each season. Between the ages of 17 to 22 we pass from adolescence to early adulthood, between those of 40 and 45 to mid-adulthood and between 60 and 65 to late adulthood. But while we may be aware in the changes taking place physically that we are passing from one season to another, at another level development may be slower or faster.

There are developmental growth tasks to be completed that are integral to passing from one season to another. The physical changes we become aware of may trick us into thinking that we have indeed left behind childhood or young adulthood, but this may not be so. Our growth

as full human persons depends upon our having learnt to trust others, our surroundings and our selves, to begin to exercise autonomy and initiative, to realise our own competence, to be faithful to our own ideals, to enter into intimacy with others, to care for others and to become coworkers with God in caring for the future of this earth.

For some this passage to maturity, to becoming a full human being may evolve naturally and smoothly. For most of us however it is likely to be a rocky passage. As an adolescent I may be crippled by a sense of inferiority, as a young adult confused as to my identity as a person, isolated from others, or I may be in mid-life struggling with the feeling that nothing is worthwhile, that too many opportunities have been lost, the wrong choices made.

Our faith journey is not separate from these seasons of our life. If a basic mistrust is what we carry with us from childhood, then we will find it harder than others to trust God, to step out in faith. If we feel inferior or incompetent, we will have difficulty believing we have gifts that God is calling us to use. If we are afraid of intimacy, we will struggle with God's invitation to us to love others, and be limited in our desire to care and to give of ourselves sacrificially. To berate ourselves for these deficiencies will do no good. What is needed is an honest recognition that I may be fifty years old, but in certain aspects my behaviour is that of an adolescent. When we can be honest in this way we are free to move on and to respond to God's invitation to become truly adult, to grow into maturity.

If we are one of these rocky evolvers, then it is likely to be a crisis that helps us move on.

These crises come most often during times of transition: from childhood to adolescence, at mid-life, at retirement and as one faces the inevitability of dying.

The following story is of a rocky evolver. I tell it at some length as it illustrates these various stages well. I suggest you read it slowly, and perhaps several times before moving on to answer the questions at the end of this section.

■ STAGE I

Mary in her late twenties told her counsellor that she had been 'a very difficult child...by nature I'm very strong-willed and very sensitive.'[2] Born in the USA in 1950, her birth came a year after her parents had married and moved from New York to a rural area where her father had grown up and felt at home. The move, however, was a hard one for her mother, who felt isolated and homesick away from the city. It seems as a result her mother unconsciously wanted to live her life through her daughter. 'She always wanted to make me in her image.' An expectation that Mary experienced negatively. 'She wanted to change

me. It seems like she's always vented her own
frustrations on me; her unhappiness, her lack of
fulfilment. It always comes out in the form of
irritation or anger or disgust towards me and the
way I do things.'

At school too Mary had difficulty with her
teachers and one in particular. She withdrew
more and more into herself, spent hours in her
bedroom alone and at times fantasised about
killing herself. The one strong relationship in
her life was with her younger brother Ron, and
at school she made other sustaining friendships.
These friendships however were disrupted when
the family moved again. This move was
disastrous for Mary.

■ STAGE 2

The next chapter of her life from seventeen to
twenty-two she describes as her 'lost or
searching years'. Caught up in the student
subculture of the sixties, she dropped out of
college and lived on the periphery. She tried
Eastern religions, pop psychology, the occult,
illicit drugs and sex. It ended this time in a real
attempt at suicide. 'I just really made a mess of

my life. But I know that in my heart I was really looking for the truth, too.'

■ STAGE 3

A change took place when at twenty-two Mary experienced a religious conversion. Her brother Ron had become a Christian and had joined a evangelical sect. Through his witness, Mary too became a Christian and joined the same sect. She was to leave after a short period, as did Ron. Now began a period when she moved from one evangelical group to another. She had a strong sense each time of God's leading her, but did not fit comfortably into any group. Often she felt herself still to be the child who could never do anything right. 'I was interpreted as being really rebellious and unsubmissive to authority - which I was in part.' Mary oscillated between extreme feelings of rejection and guilt, and a sense of God's loving her and caring for her.

At this stage in her life Mary met Harry and married him. Both had a history of felt rejection and a need for relationship. The marriage was not a success either. 'I guess I was very naive,'

Mary later told her counsellor, 'and I really wasn't a very good judge of character.'

■ STAGE 4

Aged twenty-seven, with one child and another on her way, Mary had to face the prospect of divorce. It was an agonising decision for her. 'I was really seeking the Lord as to whether to get a divorce.' Her brother, Ron, who had continued to be a strong influence in her life, helped her come to a decision. She decided as a result to move towards divorce proceedings. During this period Mary was reunited again with her parents. They invited her to come and live with them, and to bring her children with her. The group she was part of at the time opposed this on the grounds that her parents were not Christians. At this point Mary decided for herself what to do. She decided to accept her parents' invitation. She did so, and discovered that their affirmations of love for her and her children were genuine. It was at this stage that she began to think about new directions for her life, and talked with a counsellor.

The next period of her life was not an easy one for her either. She had some hard decisions to make. She began a course in computer programming, and to her surprise did extremely well. She graduated and was offered - again to her surprise- a plum job in this field. However, she continued to struggle at home with her relationship with her mother. It seemed they still could not live together harmoniously. Mary decided that it would be best for all concerned if she found a place of her own. She bought a trailer and set up home there with her two children. She had by then also begun to attend a nondenominational church, where she felt she fitted in well. Mary was surprised when her parents began to attend too. She realised she had not forfeited her relationship to them by moving out of the home. She was aware too by this stage of a change taking place in her spiritual development. 'I don't look for visions and prophecies like I used too. I feel like God does speak to me on occasion through a ... scripture. But I think on the whole, God just leads me by giving me a sense in my heart of what I ought to do, giving me a piece of what he would like me to do.'

■ COUNSELLOR'S COMMENTS

In terms of her personal development, Mary's counsellor comments that during her post-conversion period from – aged twenty-two to twenty-seven – authority for Mary was located outside of herself. It was located in a God who gave guidance and sanctioned initiatives, and in a God who came to her rescue when these initiatives didn't work out. It was not possible for Mary emotionally to question ways in which she was using God as a 'security blanket'. Authority was also located in persons on whom she depended for approval and emotional support; in particular, her brother Ron.

When her counsellor first met Mary she was a neatly dressed young woman who seemed younger than her twenty-eight years. Emotionally too she was still a hurt child seeking approval. Her sense of self kept erupting in what she expressed as her ' self-willed ways', but at the same time she craved after others' affirmation and approval. The crisis of her divorce shook her into beginning to make some decisions of her own and to trust her own judgment. She began to see that some of her earlier assumptions about her relationship to her parents were not always accurate. She began to grow up and at the same time her relationship with God began to evolve in new ways.

In this story we read of a person whose faith development was arrested by a lack in emotional development.

In what ways are you aware of your own seasons and stages? Return to your lifeline. In what ways have the various circumstances of your life helped you grow and change? How have you changed? Make some notes in answer to these questions, adding them to the appropriate phases in your lifeline.

What challenges are you facing now in terms of your development? What are the circumstances that are giving rise to these?

GROWING AND CHANGING

IN MARY WE met a woman who tried very hard to make life work, and wanted to please God. However, she was frustrated in her efforts to do so. An important turning point for her was the moment when she began to recognise some of the destructive patterns that she kept repeating, and to be able to understand why they kept recurring. At that point she had a choice - to stay bound or to break the cycle.

It is hard work to turn around and begin to move against patterns that keep us bound. It involves a commitment to grow into the true self that God sees and knows. It means coming to know ourselves, the positive and the negative sides of our personalities. None of us need fear this, for each of us is made in God's image and it is that image that we will begin to unearth, however fearful and painful this journey inward may seem at times. We each reflect a facet of

God's personality. Our 'work' in growing into our full personhood means that little by little we reflect that image more perfectly. Paul writing to the Corinthians speaks about this as 'an unveiling'. As this 'freeing' or 'unveiling' takes place, 'we can be mirrors that brightly reflect the glory of the Lord. And as the Spirit of the Lord works within us, we become more and more like him.'

Such a commitment to grow in this way is a

path to self-knowledge and self-realisation. I use these words deliberately, rather than using the term self-fulfilment. If our goal is merely to fulfil personal desires then we are going to miss our true goal, to realise the self that is our true self. On the path to self-realisation there is pain and sacrifice involved. Jesus summed this up enigmatically by telling his followers that those who wanted to save their lives must first lose them. Goethe, the German philosopher and poet, wrote in a similar vein, 'Everyone wants to be someone, but not everybody wants to grow.' If our pursuit is anything less than self-realisation we will turn away from this path, and prefer our own way to what we believe is self-fulfilment.

If we chose the path to self-realisation, we will find the path is more like a spiral, certainly not a straight line. Along the path we will become aware of wounds that need healing, diseased parts that need to be cut out, weak joints than need strengthening. We will also discover strengths we did not know we had, help that comes from beyond ourselves and aids that are a support to us in our journey. The

healing and the realisation of our true self
however will not happen all at once, but at ever
deeper levels as we trust ourselves to the healing
process in our lives.

Along this path too we will need to draw on
the wisdom, support and understanding of
others. It is not a journey that any of us should
undertake alone. We all have our blind spots
and need others to help us see them. The kind
of help we will need from others will depend
upon how wounded we are, and what kinds of
wounds.

There are all kinds of 'helps' or aids. We can
learn from our own life experiences, if we give
ourselves time to reflect on these, perhaps
through being part of a sharing or support group
or through keeping a journal. We can go on a
retreat, or workshop that will help us pursue
some area of personal growth. We can find
ourselves a spiritual director, develop new
aspects of our prayer life. We may need the help
of a professional counsellor, to undergo some
form of therapy or to learn about stress
management. Or we may need to dig a bit
deeper still through prayer for inner healing, or

psychoanalysis, or a therapeutic relationship that would enable us to feel safe enough to make this kind of journey towards wholeness.

In all this, however, it is God who is our healer. It is God who is the source of our being-at-all, and whom we meet at ever and ever deeper levels of our own being as we make this journey into becoming a whole person, fully human. This journey is hard work. God will not do it for us. He is within us and beside us, but we have to make the decision to do the work. The apostle Paul must have known this because he expressed this sense exactly: '... continue to ... work for your salvation in fear and trembling. It is God, for his own loving purpose, who puts both the will and the action into you.' (Philippians 2:13, Jerusalem Bible).

However, we always need a balance in our lives both of work and play. We look at the 'play' aspect in the next section, but before reading further complete the following exercise.

Look at the list of 'aids' in the top half of the chart on page 40. Are there some that would of help to you in your own journey? Make a note of those you would like to think more about.

Aids to Healing and Wholeness

Learning from our life-experiences, from others' responses, sharing thoughts, keeping a journal listening to God

Retreats, courses, spiritual direction, imaginative prayer

Counselling, relaxation therapy, dream therapy, art therapy, family marital and group therapy

Transactional analysis, Gestalt prayer for inner healing, psychodrama, therapeutic relationship psychanalysis, primal therapy

Requires adult (ego) strength;

God is the healer, and the source of our being

Builds up adult (ego) strength; renews, reenergises

Swimming
Cycling
Painting
Reading
Walking
Talking with friends
Watching TV
Gardening
Woodwork
Playing golf
etc.

© Carolyn Reinhart 1991

■ 6

FLOWING AND BUBBLING UP

READING, PAINTING, GARDENING, swimming. What helps you to relax, to play? What renews and energises you? If we concentrate wholly on the 'work ' of healing, we will soon run out of energy, and there will be no time or space for the new growth to root itself and grow strong. Knowing how to draw sustenance from our own inner well is essential.

Here we are touching on the very core of our spirituality. Buried deep within this well is an inner spring. It is here that we are most intimately connected to God. Jesus spoke about drinking the water that he gives us, and of that water becoming like a spring of water welling up within us . This water flows and bubbles up continually within us. From it we draw life, energy, sustenance. In the healing process we clear the spring of weeds and tangled roots. In the process of living we draw water from this spring.

Another way of describing this core is as a life force, an energy, a spark. This spark is like an electrical connection between us and God. To open ourselves to God is like turning on a switch. There is then a free flow of electricity between God and us.

These analogies, however, can only take us so far. We are not inanimate, but animate human beings, with our own wills and personalities. The connection between us and God is one of a relationship, and like any relationship grows and is nurtured by loving communication.

We communicate with God through prayer, but prayer may take many forms. The

communication is in the intention, not necessarily in the words. The way we communicate best will depend on our personality. Again we are back to the importance of knowing ourselves. The growth in understanding of the human personality that has developed in modern times helps us here. Out of this has grown a number of aids to prayer, such as the Myers Briggs Personality Type and The Enneagram; A path of self-discovery. The latter draws on insights from another spiritual tradition, that of the Sufi tradition in Islamic spirituality, although its roots are purported to go back to the influence of Christianity in Persia in the early days of the Christian Church. As a journey of self-discovery The Enneagram is increasingly being offered as one form of retreat in the programmes of Christian retreat centres.[3]

I was first introduced to the Myers Briggs Personality Type when I was lent a book called *Please understand me*.[4] I completed the test given in the book and it told me I was an introverted, intuitive and feeling type of person. In some ways I learnt nothing new, but the way in which this knowledge was presented to me helped me to assimilate it in a way that was new. Since then I have been on a number of personality type courses. These are helping me both to accept and to appreciate the kind of person I am, and have given me tools to work with in my commitment continually to be growing and maturing. An important aspect of this is in the way I now approach prayer.

Learning about prayer and personality through both Myers Briggs and Enneagram retreats has helped me understand that there broadly three ways in which we respond to the world both within and without us.

There are those of us for whom the outer world of seeing, smelling, touching, hearing and tasting – all that is outside of us – is seemingly the real world in which we live. We are in touch with this, but we may not be so in touch with our own inner world of imagination, dreams and feelings. For those of us in this category, entering our inner world through using our imagination in prayer will bring a healthy balance.

Secondly, there are those of us for whom

seemingly the real world is the inner world of our imagination, dreams and feelings. We move as others do in the outer world of cars and trees and birds, but we may not be able to name any of them. Ask us however how we feel about the noise of the traffic or the wind blowing in the trees or the singing of the birds, and we will respond at length, perhaps with a song, or a poem, or a drawing. For us, focused prayer can be helpful and bring a balance – the use in prayer of a cross or a candle or icon.

A third category is those of us who are developed to some extent in both 'worlds'. To a greater or lesser extent we move easily from one 'world' to the other, but the danger for us is that we can find ourselves at times awkwardly straddled between the two worlds, living with a constant tension. For us the prayer of quiet is essential.

Our spirit – that inner spark – is nurtured in prayer, and in other ways too. Prayer and play are closely related. Retreat givers Anne Brennan and Janice Brewi put it well: 'The rhythm of play in our life is ... deeply connected to our continual relationship to all organic life and our relationships to the events of our life and the significance of the events of our life, that is, the life of the spirit...Play allows us to be truly human, to live the rhythmic life of the spirit.'[5]

Walking, swimming, reading, painting are all ways in which I enjoy playing and which help to get me moving again when I am become bored or weary. For me they are ways to get the flow of water bubbling up again!

What is your way of praying? How has it grown and matured over the years? What form of prayer do you feel drawn to now?

What about prayer and play? Which activities refresh you and nourish your inner being? Look at the lower half of the chart on page 40. These are 'aids to healing and growth' that differing people have shared at 'inner and outer journey workshops'.[6] These aids on the lower side are those that help life to flow and bubble, and that give energy and sustenance for the next stage of the journey. Are there some here that work for you? What others would you add?

7

THE WHOLE OF LIFE

SOME YEARS AGO I wanted to discover God as a deeper reality in my life. Part of this was coming to the realisation of my own need for a greater emotional stability, particularly when under pressure. It was at this time that I began intuitively to sense that a more meditative or contemplative way of praying would be helpful. In pursuit of this I spent a few days of quiet at a Protestant retreat house in Switzerland. Those few days opened up a whole new understanding of how prayer and everyday life are closely connected.

What happened was that I realised that there were a number of changes that needed to take place in my life before I could pursue a new way of praying. I was faced with some searching questions.

Was the rhythm of each day the kind that helped me be more conscious of God's presence? Was there enough space in each day for me to do ordinary daily tasks in a way that nurtured prayer? How did I approach tasks? Did I prepare adequately, and finish what I started, or did I daily add to the disorder in my life?

Was there the right balance of work and play in my life? Did I know which activities drained me, which gave me energy. How in touch was I with my own body, its needs? Did I heed it warnings and wisdom? Did I give adequate attention to what I ate and drank, to diet and to how much exercise I needed?.

What about the physical space around me? What effect did it have on me? Were there things around me that brought warmth and colour into my life and that spoke to me of God, of friends, of purpose and of challenge?

As I began to face these questions and to make some necessary changes, I found I could enter into a new and deeper place with God in prayer. I could sit and know a stillness within that allowed me to be quiet before God and know his presence - to contemplate him. I discovered then that my intuition had been right - that this way of praying without words, or few words helped me to focus on God as my centre and to stabilise my inner life around this centre point - God within. This in turn is helping to bring the kind of rhythm and balance I need in my outer, everyday life.

This greater understanding about myself and my own needs and the importance for me of the 'prayer of quiet' came before I went on any 'personality type' courses. I have come to realise how well God knows us and if we are in touch with his movements in our life then he will lead us in the direction that brings freedom and wholeness. The work I have since done on my personality type has been a confirmation of the rightness of this approach for me, and has given

me further aids.

Pursuing my journey in this way has also had some delightful surprises for me. I have discovered again the 'playful me' and the 'creative me'. At times strong images have surfaced within the silence, a clown is one such image, another a bird in full song. Images like this have encouraged me to play more and also to give more time to creativity – painting, photography, canvas work. Discovering a way to paint freely in oils – letting scenes emerge, working with that to complete a finished painting has helped give expression to some important priorities in my life and to make some big life decisions.

In all of this there is the discovery that our spirituality is an everyday affair. It encompasses the whole of life. All parts of our person are closely connected and influence each other. If our spirituality is to be full and wholesome then we need from time to time to stop and review the way life is for us – our priorities, our plans, our life goals.

As we grow and change so our life goals grow and change.

As a young Christian I decided to put aside a career in journalism and become a full time youth club leader. If I had written down at that stage in my life what my life goal was that would have been it - to share my faith with other young people.

It was a rather a narrow life goal and I felt somewhat bereft when in my mid-thirties I began to sense that a change was in the winds, and I did not know what that change might be. Would there be any purpose in life beyond youth work!

During this present period of my life I have several such goals. They include vocational goals and others that have to do with prayer, leisure, friendships and with homemaking. One goal is to identify and explore new areas of giftedness, ones that will also be sustaining in the later part of life.

What is the balance between work and play in your life? Are you giving time for activities from both sides of the chart on page 40? What would an 'ideal day' or 'month' look like for you? What are some of your life goals?

8

SHARED PILGRIMAGE

I F THERE IS movement and growth in our life
this will be towards a greater integration of
both the inner and the outer and also the
personal and the corporate. As we have seen
none of us pursues our journey in a vacuum
sealed off from others, and to attempt to do this
is to deny our real nature. The Christian
understanding of God is that 'God is social life,
community, trinity.'[7] We cannot know God or
know ourselves apart from such a social or
community life. It is as we discover who we are
within the human community that we discover
our individuality. In some of the earlier
exercises you explored your roots in the human
community. It is likely that you also have roots
within the community of faith; that is within a
particular religious tradition. A part of you will
resonate with these roots.

John Fieldsend is a Christian minister. At the
age of nine he was parted from his family and

came to England with other Jewish children as a refugee from Nazi Germany. He was fostered by a Christian family, who shared their faith with John, but at the price of suppressing his Jewish roots. Later on he was sent by his Jewish legal guardian to a Jewish boarding school. 'I was a good Jew in term time and a good Gentile in the holidays,' he says. At the age of fifteen John chose to be baptised as a Christian rather than undergo adult initiation into the Jewish faith. 'I wish I had chosen both, ' he now shares. As an

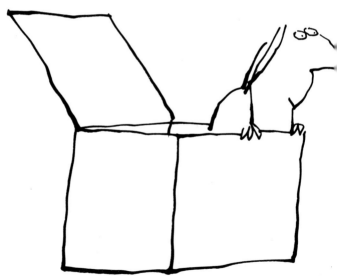

adult he had become 'totally gentilised', and later became ordained as an Anglican minister.

John married, had a family and life was happy and seemingly secure. 'Yet, somehow at the back of my mind all the time not quite knowing who I was. There were feelings and moods I couldn't really identify and cope with.' In his early forties John and his wife Elizabeth came into contact with the charismatic renewal. The lively worship they were drawn into often included Jewish melodies and dances. The music

began to stir memories in John that he had long lost touch with, and indeed had been taught early on to suppress. These stirrings led him into a painful journey that took him back to his early roots, that included counselling for healing of the memories and that also eventually led him to be reunited with the few remaining members of his family that had survived the holocaust. 'I went through and long and difficult period and came out wonderfully Jewish.' Owning his Jewish roots has deepened John's understanding of his Christian faith. He and his wife Elizabeth now belong to a Messianic Fellowship, a fellowship of Christian Jews.

To know what spiritual traditions are in our bones as it were, and also to know those to which we are drawn now and which can enrich us is essential. Each generation adds to our spiritual heritage, both in drawing from the deep well of tradition, and in adding to it new understandings and experiences. We are adding to it today in the search of many Christians throughout the world to discover an integrated spirituality that engages with all of life, and that seeks on the one hand to liberate from poverty and oppression and on the other to liberate into a new quality of life for all. The Latin American theologian Gustavo Gutierrez writes of this as giving birth to 'a distinctive way of being Christian – a spirituality.'[8] He speaks of this as 'a common enterprise. It is the passage of a people through the solitude and dangers of the desert, as it carves out its way in the following of Jesus Christ. This spiritual experience is the well from which we must drink. From it we draw the promise of resurrection.'[9]

This search for a new and distinctive way of being Christian is also giving rise to a search for a deeper prayer life, and to a contemporary exploration of Celtic, Franciscan, Ignatian and other traditional spiritualities, and also of the spiritual disciplines of other religious traditions, particularly those of the East, such as the Sufi tradition already mentioned.

All of this indicates a spiritual hunger, a hunger for reality. In our search to discover our own spirituality, we are a part of this shared pilgrimage. It is as though our inner well is part of a great network of wells which all draw inspiration from the immense ocean of who

God is. We have a common source which has many expressions. Growth comes through connecting with the ocean, not seeking to discover our own private source of water! In this search not all that emerges is authentic Christian spirituality, and what emerges needs to be tested by the community of faith against the way of Jesus himself. This is another reason for not going it alone. For this reason more and more Christians today are seeking the support of a spiritual director or soul friend, and are also meeting in small groups or Christian communities where it is possible to support others and be supported through friendship, sharing and prayer.[10]

What are your roots in the community of faith? In what ways have these nourished your journey? To what spiritual tradition are you drawn ? With whom do you meet regularly to share your experiences in the pilgrimage?. If none, how could you go about making these connections? Do you have a soul friend or spiritual director?

■ 9

CO-WORKERS WITH GOD

IN EXPLORING MY own faith journey I painted one picture that remains unfinished. It was the last one in a series of paintings and is of a path through a causeway and beyond that of a skyline. That is all.

'Hmm,' commented several friends who looked at it standing on the bookcase in my kitchen, 'that is going to be an interesting painting.' Others said more pointedly, 'When are you going to finish that?'

For a while I thought there was more detail to be added, but then I realised that the point of the painting was that it is unfinished. The view is wide open, nothing obstructing it. When I look at it I am aware both of excitement and apprehension. It speaks to me of the unknown, of the need to risk, to respond to the call of God that is always further on, beyond where I am now.

A colleague speaking to me of someone he had just met, commented sadly, 'It is as though her spirit has shrunk.' Unattended too, it is possible for our inner well to dry up, for our spirit to shrink. The lack of attention may be through indifference or busyness or caused by some disappointment or trauma that has led us to turn in on ourselves. To turn away or to turn in on ourselves is a negation of what the spiritual life is about.

In his famous icon of the Trinity the Russian

iconographer Andrei Rublev takes the ancient biblical story of the three angels that visited Abraham and Sarah in Mamre to paint a picture of the Trinity. The three travellers are seated around a table, but in such a manner that each is turned to the other. In this way the three separate persons form a circle that is a symbol of love and unity. The circle however is not closed. There is a space which draws the observer into the circle and that keeps the circle open. As we are drawn closer to God so we are drawn closer to all others and our attention becomes increasingly less centred upon ourselves and more upon the needs of others and of the earth that God has given us as our common home.

It is this movement outwards that enables us increasingly to fulfil our calling as co-workers with God in shaping the future of this earth. God has given each of us gifts and abilities to use responsibly for this purpose. He has given us the gift of imagination to envision a future that is more in keeping with what we know to be his will for all humankind, and he has given us ingenuity and skill to work with him and others to make this a reality. In the first section of this booklet we considered how parental figures and past generations have influenced our lives. We in our own turn are influencing other lives and also helping to shape the environment in which future generations will live.

The realisation that God calls us to be coworkers with him in giving birth to the new creation that he has promised is an awesome one. It touches on all aspects of our daily life. This is where 'the rub comes', as an Australian author Robert Banks puts it.

'If,' he says, ' you ask a representative sample of churchgoers whether faith and life ought to be in harmony, they will answer with a resounding 'yes'. The rub comes when you put the question in a specific way, in relation to a particular aspect of work or area of responsibility. For example, if you are a homemaker and you ask whether your religious convictions should influence the way you bring up your family and relate to your neighbours, you will probably nod your head in agreement.

'But then if I ask you whether those convictions have as clear and direct an influence on the kind of house you have, area you live in and the kind of transport you use, you will probably pause for breath.'[11]

Here we are back to decisions again. This is where we began.

Look ahead ten, then twenty, then thirty years? What kind of changes do you imagine will have taken place? What kind of world do you hope will have come into being? What kind of contribution do you feel you can make to this? Where in your life is there a need for a greater integration of faith and daily life? What decisions about this are pressing?

Take another look at the key words or phrases you started with in the first exercise. Has your understanding about what matters most to you grown or changed in working through subsequent exercises. Are there key words or phrases that you would add? Write a sentence or paragraph describing your spirituality.

■ REFERENCES

1 *Chambers Twentieth Century Dictionary*.

2 Mary's story is told in *Stages of Faith* by James W Fowler. Harper and Row, USA, 1981.

3 Further information can be obtained from the National Retreat Centre, 24 South Audley Street, London WlY 5DL.

4 David Keirsey and Marilyn Batse, *Please Understand Me Character and Temperament Types* 1978. Distributed by Prometheus Nemesis Book Conpany, CA.92014, USA.

5 Anne Brennan and Janice Brewi, *Mid Life Directions. Praying and Playing - Sources of New Dynamism* Paulist Press, 1985.

6 *Aids for Healing and Wholeness* Carolyn Reinhart, 1991. For information on 'inner and outer journey' and other retreats write to The Pastoral Centre, Post Green, 57 Dorchester Road, Lytchett Minster, Poole, Dorst BH16 6JE.

7 William McNamara, *The Human Adventure* Published Element Inc., USA, 1991.

8 Gustavo Gutierrez, *We Drink from Our Own Wells* SCM Press Ltd. 1983.

9 Ibid.

10 For information about groups in your area write to Aslan Education Unit, 36 Lower Basinghall Street, Leeds LSl 5EB.

11 Robert Banks, *All the Business of Life* Albatross Books/Lion Publishing, 1987.